Ghostly
Encounters

Kevin Walker

ROurke
Educational Media

rourkeeducationalmedia.com

Before, During, and After Reading Activities

Before Reading: Building Background Knowledge and Academic Vocabulary

"Before Reading" strategies activate prior knowledge and set a purpose for reading. Before reading a book, it is important to tap into what your child or students already know about the topic. This will help them develop their vocabulary and increase their reading comprehension.

Questions and activities to build background knowledge:
1. *Look at the cover of the book. What will this book be about?*
2. *What do you already know about the topic?*
3. *Let's study the Table of Contents. What will you learn about in the book's chapters?*
4. *What would you like to learn about this topic? Do you think you might learn about it from this book? Why or why not?*

Building Academic Vocabulary

Building academic vocabulary is critical to understanding subject content.
Assist your child or students to gain meaning of the following vocabulary words.
Content Area Vocabulary
Read the list. What do these words mean?

- *debunked*
- *existence*
- *inspires*
- *mast*
- *skeptics*
- *spiral*

During Reading: Writing Component

"During Reading" strategies help to make connections, monitor understanding, generate questions, and stay focused.
1. *While reading, write in your reading journal any questions you have or anything you do not understand.*
2. *After completing each chapter, write a summary of the chapter in your reading journal.*
3. *While reading, make connections with the text and write them in your reading journal.*
   a) *Text to Self – What does this remind me of in my life? What were my feelings when I read this?*
   b) *Text to Text – What does this remind me of in another book I've read? How is this different from other books I've read?*
   c) *Text to World – What does this remind me of in the real world? Have I heard about this before? (News, current events, school, etc....)*

After Reading: Comprehension and Extension Activity

"After Reading" strategies provide an opportunity to summarize, question, reflect, discuss, and respond to text. After reading the book, work on the following questions with your child or students to check their level of reading comprehension and content mastery.
1. How did the ghost of Elva Zona Shue help solve her own murder? *(Summarize)*
2. What are some examples of ghosts who are part of folklore? *(Infer)*
3. What is considered the most haunted house in America? *(Asking Questions)*
4. Do you believe in ghosts? Is so, what makes you believe they are real? *(Text to Self Connection)*

Extension Activity
Many families have ghost stories. Talk to your family members about ghostly encounters they have had or heard about. Create a short book by writing down all of your family ghost stories.

Table of Contents

Friendly Ghosts 4

Legendary Hauntings 10

Haunted Places 16

Memory Game 30

Index 31

Show What You Know 31

Further Reading. 31

About the Author 32

Friendly Ghosts

Abraham Lincoln is a famous American president. And a famous ghost!

Some people say he smiles as he haunts the White House!

Some ghosts are helpful. The Blue Lady reportedly haunts the seaside cliffs of California. People claim she warns children to stay away from the edge.

GHOSTLY BELIEF

Do you think ghosts are real? More than half of Americans say they believe in the **existence** of ghosts.

existence (ig-ZIS-tuhns): the fact or state of being real or alive

Elva Zona Shue helped police solve her own murder in 1897!

Police thought Elva died of natural causes. Her mother told them Elva's ghost said she was murdered. The police found Elva's husband had strangled her.

Elva Zona Shue
c. 1873 – 1897

Legendary Hauntings

Some famous ghosts aren't dead people. The *Flying Dutchman* haunts the high seas. The ghost ship is supposed to be a sign of bad luck!

GHOSTS AHOY!

There are many legends of ghost ships. People claim to see the HMS *Eurydice* off the Isle of Wight. Reports say the three-**mast** ship appears momentarily before disappearing. The ship sank in 1877.

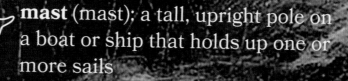

mast (mast): a tall, upright pole on a boat or ship that holds up one or more sails

In the early 19th century, the Bell family in Tennessee reported a ghost that made terrifying noises and smashed plates.

Legend has it that U.S. President Andrew Jackson visited and had strange experiences. To this day, even **skeptics** can't explain what happened.

Andrew Jackson

skeptics (SKEP-tics): people who do not accept views or opinions readily from others

According to legend, the ghost of Bloody Mary can appear anywhere. You just have to turn out the lights, look in a mirror, and say her name three times.

Of course, it is just a story made up to scare children! But the name still **inspires** fear.

FEARSOME FOLKLORE

Both the Bell Witch and Bloody Mary are part of what is called folklore. They are stories that have been passed down for generations.

inspires (in-SPIRES): fills someone with an emotion, an idea, or an attitude.

Haunted Places

Some places are famous not because of one ghost, but because they have a lot of them!

At the Moundsville Penitentiary in West Virginia, visitors say they hear the voices and steps of long-gone prisoners. Spooky!

The Moundsville Penitentiary operated from 1876 to 1995. It is now open for tours and special spooky events.

The St. Augustine Lighthouse in Florida is reportedly haunted. People hear voices and see strange shadows along the tower's **spiral** staircase.

spiral (SPYE-ruhl): winding in a continuous curve around a fixed point or central axis

The Cuban Club in Tampa, Florida, is a haunted hot spot. The elevators are said to go from floor to floor with no one inside. And visitors hear a piano playing—but no one is there!

London

In London, many people think a ghost with red eyes haunts Highgate Cemetery. Some say it's a vampire!

People have reported finding foxes in the area drained of blood. Others report seeing a floating figure passing through locked gates.

An angel statue lies on an unmarked grave in Highgate Cemetery.

In Beijing, China, locals think the Chaonei No. 81 building is haunted. Its front door is always cold. Many people report hearing voices from within.

According to legend, a construction crew almost broke a wall in Chaonei No. 81. The crew disappeared and was never heard from again.

Beijing ★

Would you spend the night on a haunted ship? The *Queen Mary* was converted into a hotel. Some report ghostly children around an empty swimming pool. Others hear screams and voices from a boiler room where a sailor died.

The RMS Queen Mary sailed from 1936 to 1967 before it was permanently moored at California's Long Beach port.

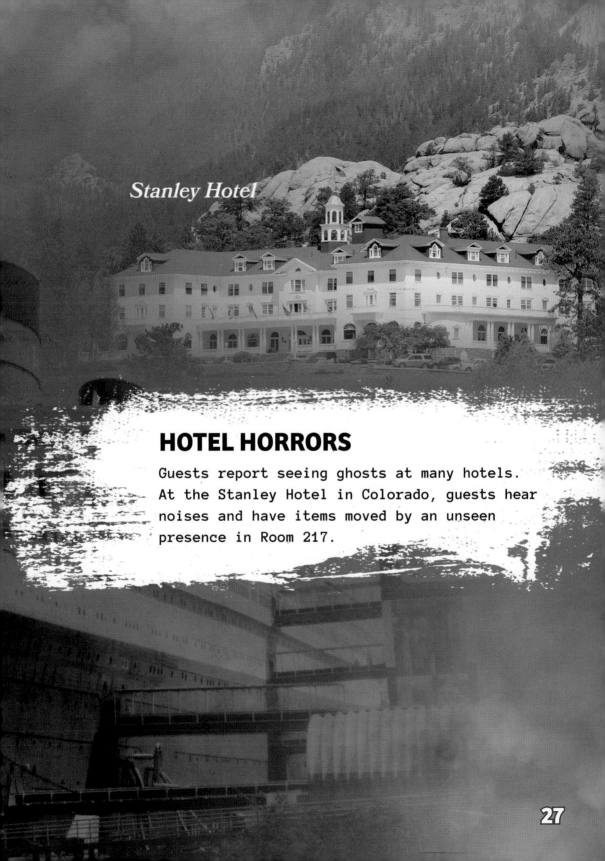

Stanley Hotel

HOTEL HORRORS

Guests report seeing ghosts at many hotels. At the Stanley Hotel in Colorado, guests hear noises and have items moved by an unseen presence in Room 217.

Some paranormal experiences can be explained. But some have not been **debunked**.

One of those is the Winchester Mystery House in San Jose, California. Many people report seeing the ghost of a former handyman. Sometimes he's even pushing a ghostly wheelbarrow!

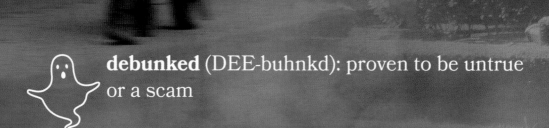

debunked (DEE-buhnkd): proven to be untrue or a scam

The Winchester mansion is said to be the most haunted house in America. It has 40 staircases and two thousand doors, some of them leading nowhere.

Memory Game

Can you match the image to what you read?

Index

Bell Witch 14

Bloody Mary 14

Chaonei No. 81 24

Cuban Club 20

Flying Dutchman 10

Lincoln, Abraham 4

Moundsville Penitentiary 16, 17

St. Augustine 18

Show What You Know

1. What former U.S. president supposedly haunts the White House?

2. Which ghost is said to have solved her own murder?

3. Where is the *Queen Mary* docked?

4. Can you name a famous haunted hotel?

5. What cemetery in London is supposedly haunted by a vampire?

Further Reading

Claybourne, Anna, *Don't Read This Book Before Bed: Thrills, Chills, and Hauntingly True Stories*, National Geographic Children's Books, 2017.

Gaiman, Neil, *The Graveyard Book*, HarperCollins, 2010.

Reynolds, Jason, *Ghost*, Atheneum/Caitlyn Dlouhy Books, 2017.

About the Author

Kevin Walker is a writer and journalist who has never seen a ghost. But his grandmother used to tell him family ghost stories that he will never forget.

Meet The Author!
www.meetREMauthors.com

www.rourkeeducationalmedia.com

PHOTO CREDITS: Cover, page1: ©Floriana Barbu; page 4, 5a, 5b, 17: ©Library of Congress; page 6, 26: ©johnnorth; page 7a: ©ilia-art; page 8: ©miljko; page 9: ©RapidEye; page 9b, 10, 13, 23a: ©Wikipedia; page11: ©FransDekkers; page 12: ©pixelfusion3D; page 12c: ©akova; page 14: ©component2; page 15a: ©JJRD; page 15b: ©StudioThreeDots; page 16a: ©naisupakit; page 16b: ©stevezmat; page 19: ©Kayann; page 20: ©FrankvandenBergh; page 21: ©Francis49; page 22: ©oorka; page 23b: ©Larry Herfindal; page 24b: ©shapecharge; page 24: ©fatido; page 25: ©DanielCase; page 26: ©EFA2015; page 27: ©RiverNorthPhotography; page 28: ©urbancow; page 29: ©BrookePierce

Edited by: Keli Sipperley
Cover and interior design by: Kathy Walsh

Library of Congress PCN Data

Ghostly Encounters / Kevin Walker
 (Unexplained)
  ISBN 978-1-64369-036-0 (hard cover)
  ISBN 978-1-64369-102-2 (soft cover)
  ISBN 978-1-64369-183-1 (e-Book)
Library of Congress Control Number: 2018955883

Rourke Educational Media
Printed in the United States of America,
North Mankato, Minnesota